Sheet Music Selections from

VOCAL • GUITAR

CONTENTS

MASTERWORKS BROADWAY

Original Broadway Cast Recording available on Masterworks Broadway.
MasterworksBroadway.com

Produced by
Alfred Music Publishing Co., Inc.
P.O. Box 10003
Van Nuys, CA 91410-0003
alfred.com

Printed in USA.

ISBN-10: 0-7390-8920-X
ISBN-13: 978-0-7390-8920-0

Cover photo: Frank Ockenfels

 Alfred Cares. Contents printed on 100% recycled paper.

LEAVE

Words and Music by
GLEN HANSARD

* Standard E frame 2nd verse.

be - fore you stood up._____
What took you so long?____

And you won't dis - ap - point me;
And the truth has a hab - it

I can do that my - self.
of fall - ing out of your mouth.

But I'm glad that you've come.
Well, now that it's come,

Now, if you don't mind,__
if you don't mind,__

Chorus:

leave,_ leave_____ and free your - self__ at the same time._
leave,_ leave_____ and please your - self__ at the same time._

Leave,_____ leave._____ Let go of my hand. You said what you had to, now

leave,_____ leave,_____ dah, dah,

dah, la la la, dah dah. La dah dah dah, la la la, dah dah. Whoa,_____

_____ la la la, dah dah. La dah dah dah, oh._____

5

Leave - 4 - 4

FALLING SLOWLY

Words and Music by
GLEN HANSARD and
MARKÉTA IRGLOVÁ

12

too   late,___   now it's gone.___

THE MOON

Words and Music by
GLEN HANSARD
Arrangement by
MARTIN LOWE

Cut the bonds___ with the moon,___ and let the dogs___ gath-er.

Burn the gauze___ in the spoon,___

and suck the poi - son up. And bleed.___ And bleed.___

The Moon - 4 - 1

IF YOU WANT ME

Words and Music by
MARKÉTA IRGLOVÁ

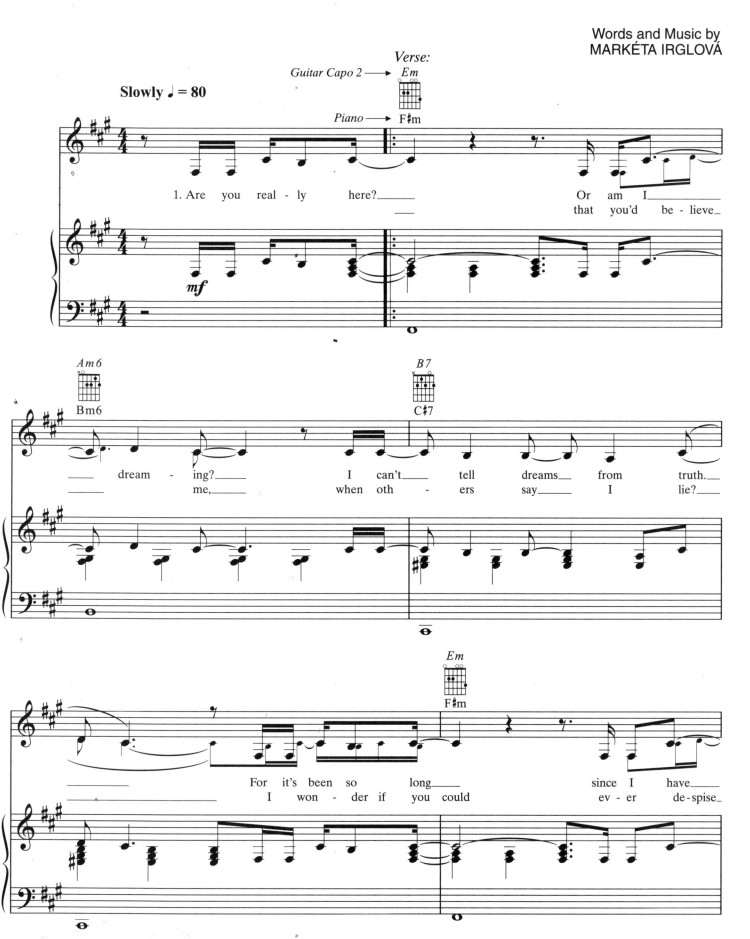

To Coda ⊕ |1.

BROKEN HEARTED HOOVER FIXER SUCKER GUY

Words and Music by
GLEN HANSARD

Verse:

Ten years a-go,___ I fell in___ love___ with an I - rish girl. She took my heart.___ But she went and screwed___ some

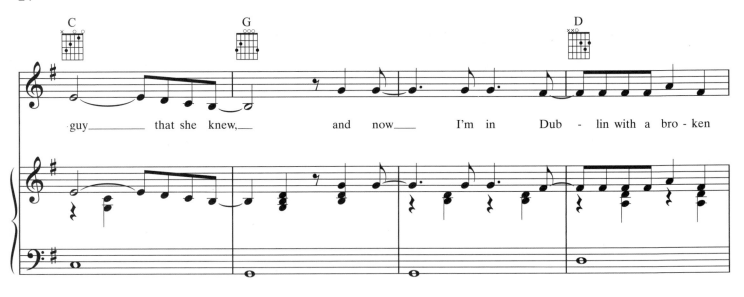

guy_____ that she knew,___ and now___ I'm in Dub - lin with a bro - ken

Moderately ♩ = 84

Chorus:

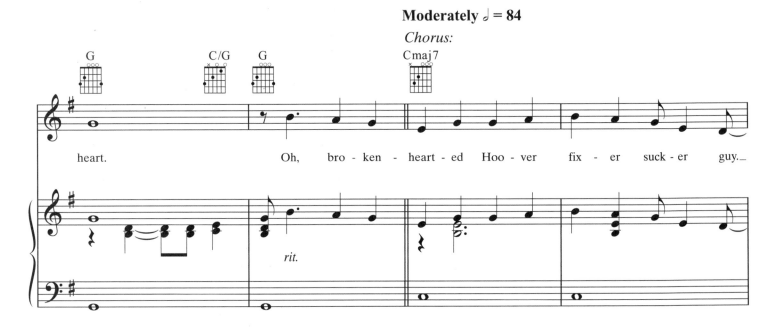

heart. Oh, bro - ken - heart - ed Hoo - ver fix - er suck - er guy._

rit.

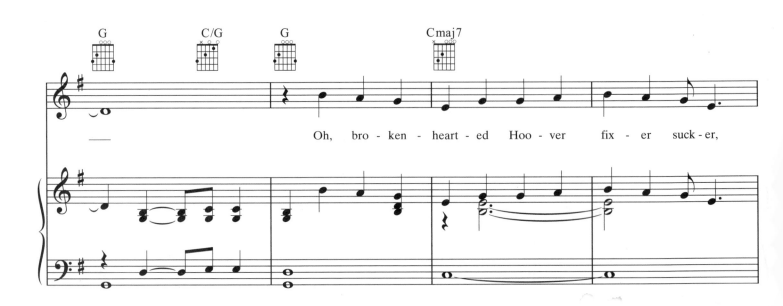

___ Oh, bro - ken - heart - ed Hoo - ver fix - er suck - er,

SAY IT TO ME NOW

Words and Music by
GLEN HANSARD, GRAHAM DOWNEY,
PAUL BRENNAN, NOREEN O'DONNELL,
COLM MACCONIOMAIRE and DAVID ODLUM

GOLD

Gtr. tuned "Open E5"

⑥ = E ③ = E
⑤ = B ②= B
④ = E ①= E

Words and Music by
FERGUS O'FARRELL

Moderately fast, in "1" (♩. = 56)

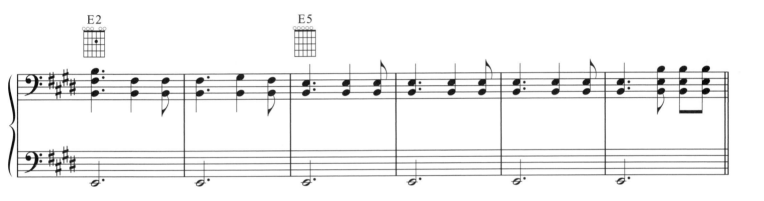

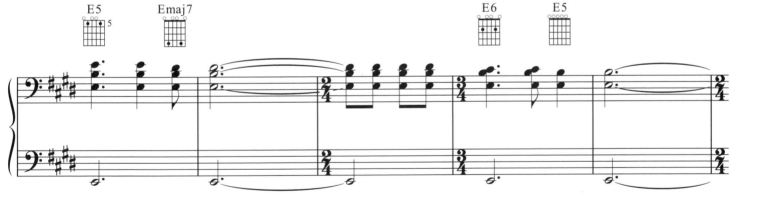

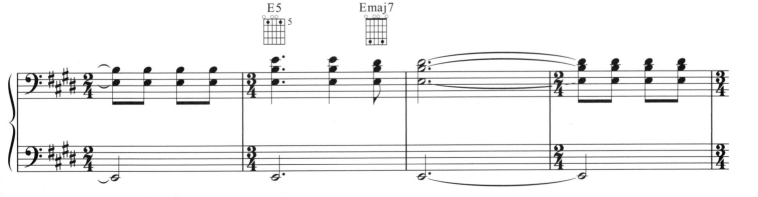

Gold - 13 - 1

32

Esus   E5   Emaj7   E6

I'm gon-na be free._____

E5   E5   Emaj7

I'm walk-ing on_____ moon - beams,_____

E6   E5   Esus   E5

_____ and star-ing out to sea.

Emaj7   E6   E5

Hey!

Gold - 13 - 11

SLEEPING

Words and Music by
GLEN HANSARD

Slowly ♩ = 69

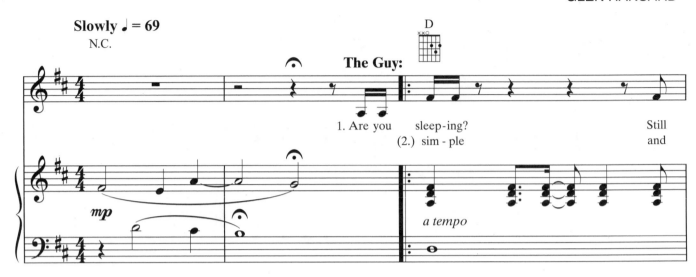

The Guy:

1. Are you sleep-ing? Still
(2.) sim - ple and

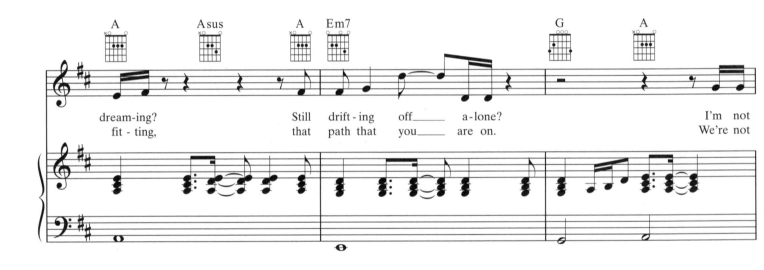

dream-ing? Still drift-ing off___ a-lone? I'm not
fit - ting, that path that you___ are on. We're not

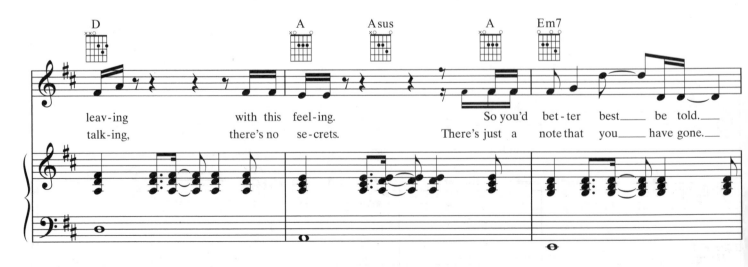

leav-ing with this feel-ing. So you'd bet-ter best___ be told.
talk-ing, there's no se-crets. There's just a note that you___ have gone.___

WHEN YOUR MIND'S MADE UP

Words and Music by
GLEN HANSARD
Vocal Arrangement by
MARTIN LOWE

Moderately bright (♩ = 160)

Guy:

So,___ ___ if you ev-er want some-thing, and you call,_____ call, then I'll come run ning___ to fight._

THE HILL

Words and Music by
MARKÉTA IRGLOVÁ

Walk-ing up the hill to-night when you have closed your

eyes. I wish I did-n't have

The Hill - 8 - 1

62

The Hill - 8 - 5

The Hill - 8 - 6

GOLD
(acapella)

Words and Music by
FERGUS O'FARRELL
Arrangement by
MARTIN LOWE

Freely (♩ = 92)

Gold - 4 - 1

68

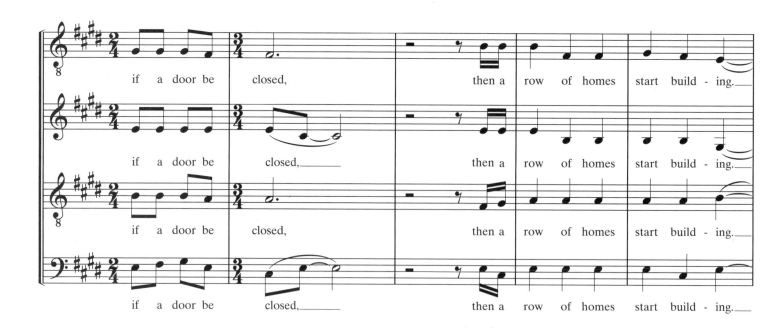

Gold - 4 - 3

And you bet-ter be you,_____ and do what you can
And you bet-ter be you,_____ and do what you can
And you bet-ter be you,_____ and do what you can
And you bet-ter be you,_____ and do what you can

do._____ When you're walk-ing on____ moon - beams____
do._____ When you're walk-ing on____ moon - beams____
do._____ When you're walk-ing on____ moon - beams____
do._____ When you're walk-ing on____ moon - beams____

and star - ing out to sea.
and star - ing out to sea.
and star - ing out to sea.
and star - ing out___ to___ sea.___

Gold - 4 - 4

FALLING SLOWLY (REPRISE)

Words and Music by
GLEN HANSARD and
MARKÉTA IRGLOVÁ

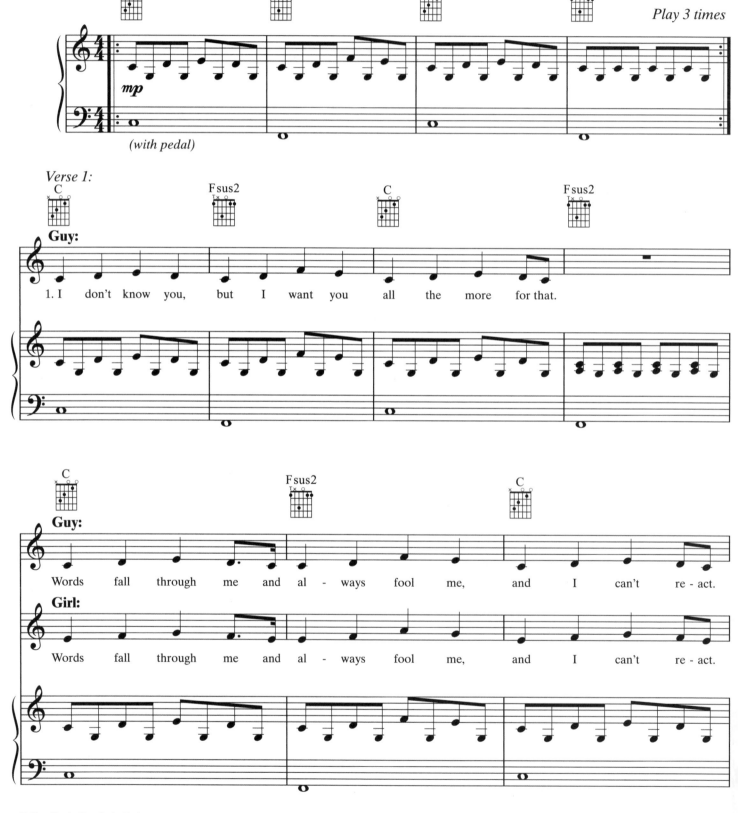

Chorus:

Oh,__ I paid__ the cost___ too   late,__   now it's gone.__

(Strings)